# Faith

# Faith

A short collection of 15 inspirational poems

First Published 2016 by Fantastic Books Publishing

Cover design and artwork by Gabi

ISBN (ebook): 978-1-909163-33-1
ISBN (paperback): 978-1-912053-68-1

## DEDICATION

This collection is dedicated to two people I've never met, John and Sam Connor.

John Connor is a poet. I first encountered his work at a friend's house. She showed me a book called Believe and told me how much it had helped her through a personal tragedy.

John Connor's verse is simple and straightforward. He tells it like it is, and clearly from the size of his following he touches the hearts of thousands. His wife Sam shared in her husband's success as a 'poet of the people' through his first two published collections, but sadly tragedy was to hit the Connors, and John's third collection, Believe III, is dedicated to the memory of his brave wife Sam who lost her battle with cancer in 2015 leaving him and their young family far too soon.

## PREFACE

Faith is a celebration of life and of the lives of loved ones lost.

Some of the poems, such as *Putting on a Show*, *Life Lives on in a Smile* and *Together Forever*, are in free verse and chart some of life's difficult journeys. They have emerged from real events and they simply tell the story of what happened, of how solace pops up from the most surprising sources, of how our world of perpetual change constantly rolls along. The quartet of *See, Hear, Speak* and *Do No Evil* was born from observation of the damage that is done when evil is perpetuated.

Some of the poems are in traditional forms. *The World, A Song for an Unknown Future* and *Counting Rowan Buds* are triolets. *Lucky in Life* and *This Perfect Life* are sestinas; and *The Corrosive "if only"* is a villanelle.

# CONTENTS

1 The World

2 Looking Back

4 Putting on a Show

6 See No Evil

7 Hear No Evil

8 Speak No Evil

9 Do No Evil

10 Together Forever

11 Life Lives on in a Smile

12 This Perfect Life

14 Life Goes On?

16 A Song for an Unknown Future

17 The Corrosive "if only"

18 Counting Rowan Buds

19 Lucky in Life

22 About the Author

# THE WORLD

With all its love and life and light,
The world's a miraculous place.
With yin and yang and fight and flight,
With all its love and life and light,
With good and evil, day and night,
With wonders everywhere you face,
With all its love and life and light,
The world's a miraculous place.

# LOOKING BACK

I look back on our time with you
And think over all the things we'd do,
Pretending the time was a rerun through
Of how I'd do it differently now.

I wouldn't shun. We wouldn't row
over trivia, and I wonder how
I didn't think back then, to plough
A different furrow with my time again.

But life's for living; not going back round
With regret at not getting that pound
of flesh from some far off bet. Feel the ground
Make the most. You've only one go through.

You loved us; it's enough to know
That you don't want our lives to slow
With regrets for moments we were low.
You loved us as we were. Enough!

Revel in memories of good, forget the rough,
The rows, deceits. Don't be tough
on yourself for me. Life's gone in a puff
of smoke. Remember me for love.

And when I've gone, don't be wholly sad,
Be thankful for the fortunate times we had.
As you want your loved ones to remember you

Without regret, remember me near or far.

We clashed a few times; who doesn't in life
It left no deep down scars of strife.
No regrets close up. None from afar.
We love each other for who we are.

# PUTTING ON A SHOW

The attack, the tragedy, the unknown fear.
It threatens, creeps closer, then it's here!
It fills your head, your heart, your time,
Puts life on hold, steals peace of mind.
Corrosive acid, eating away
At the fabric of your every day.
No respite, no way out, no slack
From the millstone sitting on your back.

Then someone asks to lean on you.
A friend, a child, someone who
has no concern for your millstone.
They're too engrossed in one of their own.
You show them strength; though it's just a show.
You flex your muscles, pretend to grow.

Because not everyone's in the know,
Your strength looks real to casual eyes.
There's a funny consolation in disguise.
How odd. It's worth the effort to meet
the world with this deceit.
It somehow keeps the worst at bay,
Gets you through another day.

The time will come when the mask can drop,
And show you're nowhere near the top
of the slippery slope but way down low,
Ready to answer, Can you cope?

With a truthful, No.

When the day comes, there's a bolt from the blue.
You dig to the very depths of You
To pull out a remnant of despair,
A poor relation to the fiend that was there,
Not enough left to engender fear.

You're over it, round it, on top of it, past it.
Its power has gone. You've moved on.
The loss of the secret so long kept,
Will give you pause before you can accept
That time and faith have let you heal,
And behind the façade the strength is real.

# SEE NO EVIL

See no evil is harder to do than say,
With so much wrong in the world today.
Why not see evil if it's there?
Seek it out with glimpse and stare.
And now I see it everywhere.
The evil turns my mind, my gut,
Because now I'm seeing nothing but.
Yet in this world it's never quite
Cut and dried, black and white.
See no evil? Not quite that.
Understand what's there, but always know
That where there's evil, good can grow.
Starve the evil shoots of focus,
Nurture the tiniest particle of good.
See an abundant garden grow
Where once a barren wilderness stood.

# HEAR NO EVIL

Hear no evil is easier to say,
Than to act on in the world today.
So with this enemy all around,
Let's learn to know it by its sound.
But when you hear it everywhere,
Its evil sounds will twist your gut,
Your ears filled with nothing but
Vile curses, blasphemies of sin,
Without the space to let good in.
Hear no evil? Not quite that.
Understand that evil's there, but know
That where there's evil, good can grow.
Ignore the curse and its fake lustre.
Recognise when it's only bluster.
Evil words cry out for notice.
Snub them with disregard, and cherish
The whispered blessings that need light to flourish.
Watch them grow and make their mark.
Overwhelming as they grow,
And evil shrivels in the dark.

# SPEAK NO EVIL

Speak no evil is easier to say,
Than it is to do in the world today.
When evil speaks it lights the fire
To meet the fiery words with ire.
And now I speak it all the time.
It twists my gut and turns my mind,
Because now I'm speaking nothing but.
Yet it's never all one side,
Black and white or cut and dried.
Speak no evil? Not quite that.
Use harsh words wisely, know they hide
A spark of good somewhere inside.
Feed the good words drop by drop.
Neglect the bad and let them rot.
Watch good grow tall, a bumper crop.

# DO NO EVIL

To do no evil is easier to say,
Than to act on in the world today.
With evil raging all around
Why not fight on evil's ground?
But now I'm in thrall to evil deeds.
They fill my world; they quench my needs.
And now the world's an evil place,
Where sin is profit, good is gone
from within, and evil's won.
Or has it? Nothing's quite so clear
As tabloid headlines shout aloud,
Bolstering profit with rising fear.
No, nothing's ever quite that clear.
Do no evil? Not quite that.
Be aware but don't be drawn
To nurture evil deeds, be sworn
To recognize the good, the spark
That glints from deep within the dark.
Watch it kindle, snap and glow,
Catch light and then begin to grow.

# TOGETHER FOREVER

I feel broken, empty, nothing to give,
Hurled to the stars. How can I live?
When you're not in the world.
We loved for too long, for it to be gone.
It's everywhere, it's here, it's there,
In memories, mementos, tiny reminders
that no one can see, just you and me.
In huge yawning caverns of grief
That gape their jaws beyond belief.
We loved for too long, for it to be gone.

Who is speaking in my ear?
Whispers that only I can hear.
Was that a bird that just took flight,
Or someone waiting out of sight?

You haven't left, you just went out.
Back in a jiffy without a doubt.
I'll smile again. I know you're near.
We loved for too long, for it to be gone.
You haven't gone. You're here.

## LIFE LIVES ON IN A SMILE

Not a giggle, not a smile, just half a thing
that moves my face unbidden as I watch a baby grin,
watch kittens play, chasing bugs in new-mown hay,
a robin puffing out its chest to sing.
The smile starts out as half a thing
that grows at memories of you,
at how you would have smiled too,
to see the baby laugh, the kittens play,
chasing bugs in new-mown hay,
the robin chirping on the tree,
within a spit of you and me.
The smile finds its other half,
grows wider still, becomes a laugh.
No matter who, no matter where,
We shared so much, it's always there
It's always ours, for us to share.

# THIS PERFECT LIFE

Into a life we hadn't known was perfect,
A hint of something wrong.
A seed of doubt begins to grow.
We hear the diagnosis.
Wanting - expecting – reassurance,
But no. It's a death sentence.

The shock of the terminal sentence
Rocks a life that was suddenly perfect,
But for this bombshell, this monstrous
wound, we'd seen nothing wrong.
This cruel diagnosis
That leaves us with nowhere to go.

No choice but to follow the flow,
Rush on to the end of the sentence,
As determined by the diagnosis.
The life we hadn't known was perfect
Has shifted, somehow gone off song,
And strangely in that is reassurance.

A phony war type of reassurance,
But still a comfort to know
That what was irreparably wrong
Has become a lesser sentence,
Now we know that life was perfect
Before the diagnosis.

Now life subsumes diagnosis
And builds its own reassurance.

A perfect life is no less perfect
For knowing what we now know.
It doesn't lift the death sentence,
But it dilutes the wrong.

What was right doesn't turn wrong,
Just through a diagnosis,
With its accompanying sentence.
The realisation is reassurance
And allows the certainty to grow
About the life we didn't know was perfect.

Now we have the reassurance
To be fortunate enough to know
That life, though shortened now, is perfect.

# LIFE GOES ON?

Life goes on? Well, that's a lie.
When you left the world, it shattered,
Smashed in pieces, left life itself to die.
Yet even damaged as it was,
It somehow failed to stop.
The fragments slid together painfully and slow.
I resented them for being there.
They should shatter and go.
Pieces clicked together, making life roll on.
Go on without me, I told it, if you must go on.
But it carried me, pushed me, though unwilling,
I never wanted it and gave no permission.
My journey stopped when the world lost you.
I screamed, I cried … I fought … resented.
It dragged me on like a thing demented,
The crest of an unrelenting wave.
It kept me just above the surface,
Made me look around, see change, see progress.
Had I stopped crying? Did I laugh?
I can't have moved along without you.
And I didn't. You were there.
You smiled with me at memories only we could share.
You laughed with me at in-jokes.
You shared my anger at some incidental ranting TV politician.
You aren't lost to me. Life didn't die.
You were there.
You were with me every step.
'Life goes on' has lost its lie.

# A SONG FOR AN UNKNOWN FUTURE

A song that has still to be sung,
From a choir that's yet to exist.
A concert from places far flung.
A song that has still to be sung,
From voices yet to give tongue,
Minds that can't grasp the gist
Of a song that has still to be sung,
From a choir that's yet to exist.

# THE CORROSIVE "IF ONLY"

The corrosive *"if only"* – a trap,
A mind-eater, memory tap.
Take life by the scruff and fulfil it.

Don't let regrets drown and kill it.
If a doubt pushes up, then still it.
The corrosive *"if only"* – a trap.

Let memory in as a comforting wrap,
For warm reminiscence and a soothing nap.
Take life by the scruff and fulfil it.

Take all of your being and fill it
With good times to comfort and thrill it.
The corrosive *"if only"* – a trap.

Let real thoughts lie in your lap.
Good times are the routes on your map.
The corrosive *"if only"* – a trap.
Take life by the scruff and fulfil it.

## COUNTING ROWAN BUDS

Sitting in the garden as the sun goes down,
Counting rowan buds reaching for the sky,
As the birds sing and the hedgerows sigh.
Sitting in the garden as the sun goes down,
With the blossom bursting all around.
It's where my mother's ashes lie.
Sitting in this garden as the sun goes down,
Counting rowan buds reaching for the sky.

## LUCKY IN LIFE

How lucky are we,
With this love of life?
Sure, nothing's forever,
But to know we've known love,
To know we've known peace,
Is fortune indeed.

Yes, it's fortune indeed,
To know that we're free,
To have lived life in peace,
Without serious strife.
To have known true love,
To know it's forever.

Is anything forever?
Perhaps not in deed,
But it must be in love,
Which is all that we see
As the foundation of life,
For as long as the lease.

It's a lifetime this lease,
As good as forever.
It's what it's for, life.
It's best to take heed.
Would you want to be free

From the shackles of love?

The shackles of love
Could generate peace,
Far wider than we see,
As long as forever.
It's a long time indeed
But worth it for life.

A long and fortunate life
That's bounded by love,
Is true fortune, indeed.
With calm sailing and peace,
Be thankful forever
For the life that you see.

The life you and me
Live together forever
In fortune and peace.

# ABOUT THE AUTHOR

Christian Danvers has been a poet all his life, but this is his first published collection. He loves life and has celebrated it in his writing since he was old enough to hold a pen. He thinks the technological advances of the modern world are truly wonderful, and has an ambition one day to understand what it's all about. Until then, if things get too confusing he simply retreats to the world of human nature that, for good or evil, never loses the security of familiarity.